A Little Golden Book® Biography

For Mom, my dancing queen —J.D.

A GOLDEN BOOK • NEW YORK

Golden Books
An imprint of Random House Children's Books
A division of Penguin Random House LLC
1745 Broadway, New York, NY 10019
penguinrandomhouse.com
rhcbooks.com

Library of Congress Control Number: 2024952491
ISBN 978-0-593-90448-0 (trade) — ISBN 978-0-593-90449-7 (ebook)
Manufactured in the United States of America
10 9 8 7 6 5 4 3 2 1
EU Contact: Penguin Random House Ireland, 32 Nassau Street, Dublin D02 YH68.
https://eu-contact.penguin.ie

ABBA

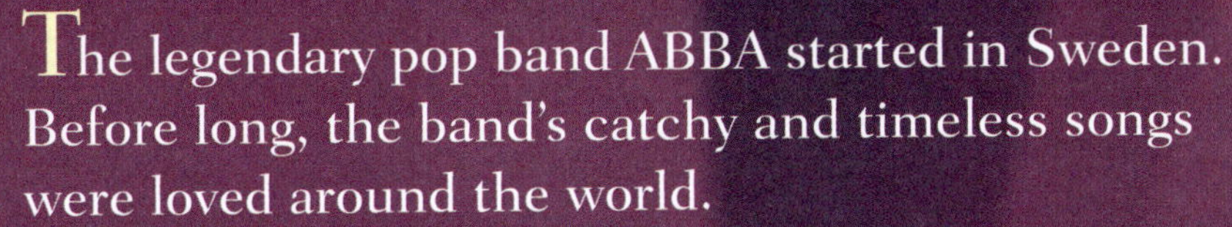

The legendary pop band ABBA started in Sweden. Before long, the band's catchy and timeless songs were loved around the world.

The performers—Agnetha, Björn, Benny, and Anni-Frid—were all successful musicians before they met and formed ABBA.

Björn Ulvaeus was born on April 25, 1945. As a child, he listened to rock and roll music. When he was eleven, his parents bought him a guitar, and he quickly began writing his own songs.

In high school, Björn and three friends formed a band called the Hootenanny Singers. The popular folk group toured throughout Sweden and had many hits.

Anni-Frid Lyngstad was born on November 15, 1945, in Norway. Everyone called her Frida. When she was a baby, she and her grandmother moved to Sweden. Her grandmother taught her traditional Norwegian folk songs.

As a teenager, Frida sang with different bands. In 1967, she entered a talent competition and won. The first prize was a recording contract. She also got to perform on live TV. People all over Sweden heard her sing!

Benny Andersson was born on December 16, 1946. He grew up surrounded by music. From the age of six, he played accordion with his father and grandfather. When he was ten, his parents got him a piano and he taught himself how to play.

In 1964, Benny joined the band Hep Stars as a keyboardist. They soon became the biggest pop band in Sweden!

Agnetha Fältskog was born on April 5, 1950. As a young girl, she enjoyed singing and playing the piano. She was also in the church choir.

When Agnetha was seventeen, she wrote and recorded a song called "Jag var så kär" ("I Was So in Love"). It caught the attention of a producer, and he offered her a record deal. The next year, the song was at the top of the Swedish charts.

Björn and Benny met when their bands were on tour. They discovered they both had an interest in songwriting.

Soon, they teamed up to write songs for each other's bands as well as other Swedish singers. By 1970, the two friends were writing and performing their own songs as a duo under the name Björn & Benny.

Björn, Agnetha, Frida, and Benny all met thanks to their work in the music industry. Before long, love was in the air! Björn married Agnetha, and Benny married Frida.

The couples were good friends and spent a lot of time together at Björn and Agnetha's cabin on Viggsö, an island off the coast of Sweden. Agnetha and Frida sometimes sang background vocals on Benny and Björn's records. Their singing voices complemented one another perfectly.

With Benny and Björn's songwriting skills, and Agnetha and Frida's beautiful harmonies, the couples noticed they had something special. It wasn't long before they decided to form their own band. Originally, they called themselves Björn & Benny, Agnetha & Anni-Frid, but they decided to use the first letter of each of their names to create ABBA.

In 1973, the band entered an international competition called the Eurovision Song Contest. They sang "Ring Ring," a song from their first album, and came in third place. The next year, they entered the contest again and sang "Waterloo." With their dazzling costumes, matching dance moves, and upbeat music, they wowed the crowd—and the judges. ABBA won!

After their victory, ABBA went on tour. Soon, "Waterloo" was a hit, not only in Sweden but across the world. The band had finally made it big!

However, not all the reviews were positive. Many people didn't like ABBA's outfits. Critics thought the band was a one-hit wonder. Some radio stations refused to play their songs. But none of this stopped ABBA fans from buying their records!

In 1975, the band released an album called *ABBA* and proved the critics wrong. Three songs from the album—"I Do, I Do, I Do," "SOS," and "Mamma Mia"—went to the top of the charts!

And ABBA didn't stop! Their next album, *Arrival*, had even more popular songs, including "Dancing Queen." The disco hit was played everywhere! People couldn't help but dance and sing along whenever they heard it.

ABBA became known for their unique costumes. Whether on tour or in videos, you could expect to see bright colors, platform boots, and lots of sparkling sequins. They always put on a spectacular show!

ABBA was one of the most famous bands in the world. But by 1981, things began to change for the group. Both couples had ended their marriages, and the band struggled to stay together.

They continued to create music for a while, but after a performance on December 11, 1982, Björn, Benny, Agnetha, and Frida decided to go their separate ways.

ABBA's music, however, was here to stay. In 1992, *ABBA Gold: Greatest Hits* was released. It was ABBA's highest-selling album, and one of the best-selling albums of all time.

In 1999, ABBA's music was used in the stage musical *Mamma Mia!* The popular show was later adapted into a movie. A sequel called *Mamma Mia! Here We Go Again* came out in 2018. Benny and Björn even had cameos in the film!

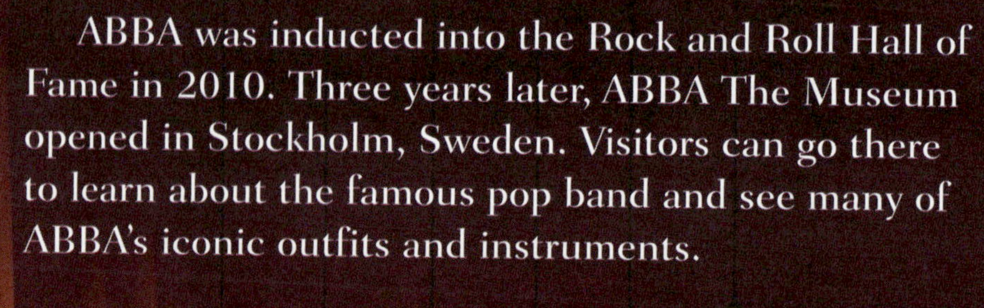

ABBA was inducted into the Rock and Roll Hall of Fame in 2010. Three years later, ABBA The Museum opened in Stockholm, Sweden. Visitors can go there to learn about the famous pop band and see many of ABBA's iconic outfits and instruments.

In 2021, almost fifty years after ABBA began, Benny, Björn, Agnetha, and Frida reunited to release another album called *Voyage*. Fans old and new enjoyed listening to ABBA's latest music. And once again, the album topped the charts around the world!

ABBA is considered one of the greatest pop groups of all time. Their memorable melodies and lyrics still make people want to get up and dance! For that, ABBA's fans all say, "Thank you for the music!"